# Teacher Edition

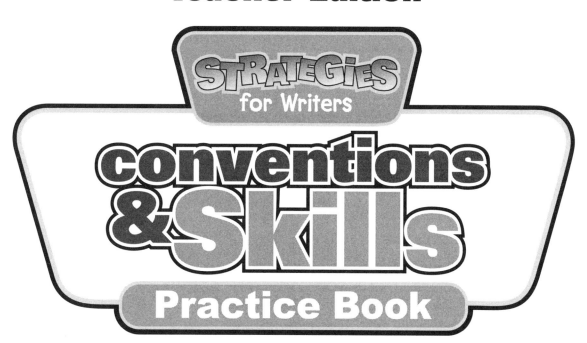

STRATEGIES for Writers

conventions &Skills

Practice Book

## Level B

D1716626

## Authors

**Leslie W. Crawford, Ed.D.**
Georgia College & State University

**Rebecca Bowers Sipe, Ed.D.**
Eastern Michigan University

**Robert C. Calfee, Ph.D.**
University of California, Riverside

**Editorial Development by** Cottage Communications

**Cover Design by** Tommaso Design Group

**Production by** Marilyn Rodgers Bahney Paselsky

Copyright © Zaner-Bloser, Inc.

Zaner-Bloser, Inc., P.O. Box 16764, Columbus, Ohio 43216-6764 (1-800-421-3018)

ISBN 0-7367-1843-5

Printed in the United States of America
       04   05   06   106  5  4  3  2

# Table of Contents

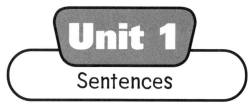

## Unit 1
### Sentences

**Lesson 1** What Is a Sentence? . . . . . . . . . . . . . . . . . . . . .7

**Lesson 2** Complete Subject and Complete Predicate . . . . . .9

**Lesson 3** Simple Subject . . . . . . . . . . . . . . . . . . . . . . . .11

**Lesson 4** Simple Predicate . . . . . . . . . . . . . . . . . . . . . . .13

**Lesson 5** Sentence Fragments . . . . . . . . . . . . . . . . . . . .15

**Lesson 6** Sentences That Tell . . . . . . . . . . . . . . . . . . . .17

**Lesson 7** Sentences That Ask . . . . . . . . . . . . . . . . . . . .19

**Lesson 8** Telling or Asking Sentences . . . . . . . . . . . . . . .21

**Lesson 9** Sentences That Command . . . . . . . . . . . . . . . .23

**Lesson 10** Sentences That Show Strong Feelings . . . . . . . . . .25

## Unit 2
### Parts of Speech

**Lesson 11** Nouns . . . . . . . . . . . . . . . . . . . . . . . . . . . .27

**Lesson 12** Proper Nouns . . . . . . . . . . . . . . . . . . . . . . . .29

**Lesson 13** Common Nouns and Proper Nouns . . . . . . . . . . . .31

**Lesson 14** Singular and Plural Nouns . . . . . . . . . . . . . . . .33

**Lesson 15** Action Verbs . . . . . . . . . . . . . . . . . . . . . . . .35

**Lesson 16** Verbs That Tell About the Past . . . . . . . . . . . . .37

**Lesson 17** Noun or Verb . . . . . . . . . . . . . . . . . . . . . . . .39

**Lesson 18** Adjectives That Tell How Many . . . . . . . . . . . . .41

**Lesson 19** Other Adjectives . . . . . . . . . . . . . . . . . . . . . .43

**Lesson 20** *And, Or, But* . . . . . . . . . . . . . . . . . . . . . . . .45

## Unit 3
### Usage

**Lesson 21** *Its* and *It's* . . . . . . . . . . . . . . . . . . . . . . . . **47**

**Lesson 22** *Its* and *It's* . . . . . . . . . . . . . . . . . . . . . . . . .49

**Lesson 23** *A* and *An* . . . . . . . . . . . . . . . . . . . . . . . . .51

**Lesson 24** *Their* and *They're* . . . . . . . . . . . . . . . . . . .53

**Lesson 25** *They're* and *There* . . . . . . . . . . . . . . . . . . .55

**Lesson 26** *Their, There,* and *They're* . . . . . . . . . . . . . .57

**Lesson 27** The Verb *Go* . . . . . . . . . . . . . . . . . . . . . . .59

**Lesson 28** The Verb *Eat* . . . . . . . . . . . . . . . . . . . . . . . 61

**Lesson 29** The Verb *Come* . . . . . . . . . . . . . . . . . . . . .63

**Lesson 30** The Verb *Give* . . . . . . . . . . . . . . . . . . . . . .65

## Unit 4
### Grammar

**Lesson 31** Making the Subject and Verb Agree . . . . . . . . . . .67

**Lesson 32** More Practice in Making Subjects and Verbs Agree . .69

**Lesson 33** Forms of the Verb *Be* . . . . . . . . . . . . . . . . . .71

**Lesson 34** Verbs That Tell About the Past . . . . . . . . . . . . .73

**Lesson 35** Choosing the Correct Verb Tense . . . . . . . . . . . .75

**Lesson 36** Subject Pronouns . . . . . . . . . . . . . . . . . . . . .77

**Lesson 37** Object Pronouns . . . . . . . . . . . . . . . . . . . . . .79

**Lesson 38** Choosing the Correct Pronoun . . . . . . . . . . . . . .81

**Lesson 39** Using *I* or *Me* With Another Name . . . . . . . . . .83

**Lesson 40** Comparing With Adjectives . . . . . . . . . . . . . . . .85

## Unit 5
### Mechanics

**Lesson 41** Capitalizing the First Word in a Sentence . . . . . . . .87
**Lesson 42** Periods and Question Marks . . . . . . . . . . . . . . .89
**Lesson 43** Periods and Exclamation Points . . . . . . . . . . . .91
**Lesson 44** Proper Nouns . . . . . . . . . . . . . . . . . . . . .93
**Lesson 45** Abbreviations . . . . . . . . . . . . . . . . . . . . .95
**Lesson 46** Contractions . . . . . . . . . . . . . . . . . . . . .97
**Lesson 47** Writing Sentences Correctly . . . . . . . . . . . . . .99
**Lesson 48** Commas in a Series . . . . . . . . . . . . . . . . . .101
**Lesson 49** Quotation Marks . . . . . . . . . . . . . . . . . . .103
**Lesson 50** Book Titles . . . . . . . . . . . . . . . . . . . . . .105


**Index of Skills** . . . . . . . . . . . . . . . . . . . . . . . . . . .107
**Index of Topics** . . . . . . . . . . . . . . . . . . . . . . . . . .109

# What Is a Sentence?

## Learn

**a.** George Washington Carver was a scientist and a teacher.

**b.** Lived long ago.

Which group of words tells a complete thought, **a.** or **b.**? _____ a.

> A **sentence** is a group of words that tells one complete thought. It begins with a capital letter. It ends with an end mark.

## Practice

Circle **S** if the group of words is a complete sentence. Write a period after each sentence. Circle **NS** if the group of words is not a complete sentence.

**1.** George Washington Carver in 1864 _____        S    (NS)

**2.** His parents were slaves __.__        (S)    NS

**3.** They lived on a farm __.__        (S)    NS

**4.** Carver helped Southern farmers __.__        (S)    NS

**5.** Interested in plants and peanuts _____        S    (NS)

**6.** He invented new things to make from peanuts __.__        (S)    NS

*Strategies for Writers—Conventions & Skills Practice*    Unit 1    **7**

# Apply

Decide which word or group of words in the Word Bank will complete each sentence. Write the words on the line. Then read your sentence to make sure it is a complete thought. Be sure to begin each sentence with a capital letter.

## Word Bank

was important to farming          He
Southern farmers                  This man
made peanut products              lived on a farm

Answers may vary. Possible answers appear below.

**7.** Young George ___lived on a farm___.

**8.** ___He/This man___ studied peanuts and other plants.

**9.** Later, Carver ___made peanut products___.

**10.** ___Southern farmers___ decided to grow more peanuts.

**11.** ___He/This man___ showed farmers better ways to use their land.

**12.** George Washington Carver ___was important to farming___.

*Strategies for Writers*—Conventions & Skills Practice   Unit 1

# Complete Subject and Complete Predicate

## Learn

**a.** Elizabeth Blackwell / was the first American woman doctor.

**b.** She/faced many problems.

In sentence **a.**, the complete subject and the complete predicate are separated by a slash (/). Draw a slash to separate the complete subject and the complete predicate in sentence **b.**

> The **complete subject** of a sentence tells whom or what the sentence is about. The **complete predicate** tells what the subject does or is.

## Practice

Read each sentence. Circle **S** if the underlined word or words are the complete subject. Circle **P** if the underlined words are the complete predicate.

**1.** <u>Women</u> could not be doctors long ago.  (S)  P

**2.** Elizabeth Blackwell <u>wanted to be a doctor.</u>  S  (P)

**3.** Medical schools <u>would not let her in.</u>  S  (P)

**4.** <u>One school</u> took her as a joke.  (S)  P

**5.** She <u>was the only woman student there.</u>  S  (P)

**6.** <u>She</u> soon became a doctor.  (S)  P

# Apply

Write a complete subject from the Word Bank to complete each sentence. Be sure to begin each sentence with a capital letter.

## Word Bank

| | |
|---|---|
| Elizabeth Blackwell | Many patients |
| Hospitals | She |
| Many women | This pioneer |

**Answers may vary. Possible answers appear below.**

7. _____ **Elizabeth Blackwell** _____ got her degree in 1849.

8. _____ **Hospitals** _____ would not hire her.

9. _____ **She** _____ started a school for women.

10. _____ **This pioneer** _____ is a hero to women today.

11. _____ **Many women** _____ are doctors now.

12. _____ **Many patients** _____ have a woman doctor today.

Copyright © Zaner-Bloser, Inc.

Name _____

# Simple Subject

## Learn

Farm workers had help from Cesar Chavez.

The complete subject is underlined in this sentence. _____

Which underlined word is the most important one? _____ **workers** _____

> The complete subject is made up of all the words that tell about the subject. The **simple subject** is the most important word or words in the complete subject.

## Practice

The complete subject of each sentence is underlined.
Draw a circle around each simple subject.

**1.** (Cesar Chavez) was born in Arizona in 1927.

**2.** His (parents) were migrant workers.

**3.** Migrant (workers) move from farm to farm.

**4.** The (workers) pick crops on large farms.

**5.** These (people) earned very little money.

**6.** Farm (owners) didn't pay workers well.

# Apply

For each sentence, choose a simple subject from the Word Bank. Write it on the line to complete each sentence. Be sure to begin each sentence with a capital letter.

## Word Bank

| | |
|---|---|
| group | Cesar Chavez |
| customers | workers |
| owners | People |

**Answers may vary. Possible answers appear below.**

7. _____ People _____ working on farms needed help.

8. _____ Cesar Chavez _____ helped workers become a group.

9. The _____ group _____ asked customers not to buy some crops.

10. Many _____ customers _____ stopped buying those crops.

11. The farm _____ owners _____ had to pay the workers more money.

12. Now migrant _____ workers _____ make more money.

# Simple Predicate

## Learn

Mary McLeod Bethune (started) a school with just $1.50.

The complete predicate is underlined in this sentence.

Circle the underlined word that tells what Ms. Bethune did.

> The complete predicate tells what the subject is or does. The **simple predicate** is the most important word in the predicate. The simple predicate is a verb.

## Practice

The complete predicate is underlined in each sentence. Draw a circle around the simple predicate.

**1.** Mary McLeod Bethune (lived) a long time ago.

**2.** She (grew) up in South Carolina.

**3.** Later, she (moved) from her home.

**4.** Bethune (became) a teacher.

**5.** She (began) a school for black children in Florida.

**6.** Five girls (went) to her school at first.

# Apply

For each sentence, choose a simple predicate from the Word Bank. Write it on the line to complete each sentence.

## Word Bank

| listened | had | worked |
|----------|-----|--------|
| became | added | started |

**Answers may vary. Possible answers appear below.**

**7.** Bethune's small school soon _____**had**_____ many students.

**8.** Later, Bethune _____**added**_____ a high school.

**9.** She even _____**started**_____ a college.

**10.** She _____**became**_____ a national leader.

**II.** Mary McLeod Bethune _____**worked**_____ with three presidents.

**12.** They all _____**listened**_____ to her ideas.

# Sentence Fragments

## Learn

**a.** Long ago, women had few rights.

**b.** Worked hard for their rights.

Which group of words is not a complete thought, **a.** or **b.**? ___ **b.** ___

> A **sentence fragment** is a group of words that does not tell a complete thought. A fragment might be missing a subject or a predicate. Do not use a fragment as a sentence.

## Practice

Circle **S** if the group of words is a complete sentence. Write a period at the end of each sentence. Circle **NS** if the group of words is not a sentence.

**1.** Lucretia Mott was born in 1793 __.__      (S)      NS

**2.** Against slavery ____      S      (NS)

**3.** Went to a meeting about slavery ____      S      (NS)

**4.** She was not allowed into the meeting __.__      (S)      NS

**5.** No women there ____      S      (NS)

**6.** Knew it was wrong ____      S      (NS)

*Strategies for Writers—Conventions & Skills Practice*   Unit 1

# Apply

Read each sentence fragment. Write **S** if it is missing a subject. Write **P** if it is missing a predicate. Then choose the missing part from the Word Bank. Write it on the line to complete the sentence. Be sure to begin each sentence with a capital letter.

## Word Bank

got half men's pay
Lucretia Mott
became a leader

Women
was unfair
have more rights

**Answers may vary. Possible answers appear below.**

7. _____Lucretia Mott_____ was once a teacher. **S**

8. Back then, women teachers _____got half men's pay_____. **P**

9. This low pay _____was unfair_____. **P**

10. _____Women_____ worked to get fair pay and other rights. **S**

11. Lucretia Mott _____became a leader_____. **P**

12. Now, women _____have more rights_____. **P**

*Strategies for Writers—Conventions & Skills Practice* Unit I

# Sentences That Tell

## Learn

**a.** Have you heard of Frederick Jones?

**b.** He invented a way to keep food cold in trucks.

Which sentence tells you something, **a.** or **b.**?    **b.**

> A **telling sentence** makes a statement. It ends with a period. An **asking sentence** asks a question. It ends with a question mark.

## Practice

If the sentence is a telling sentence, circle **T**. If the sentence is an asking sentence, circle **A**. Write a period (**.**) at the end of each telling sentence. Write a question mark (**?**) at the end of each asking sentence.

**1.** Did Frederick Jones go to college __?__          T    (A)

**2.** Frederick Jones was born in 1893 __.__          (T)    A

**3.** Did many colleges take black people then __?__          T    (A)

**4.** Few colleges took black people then __.__          (T)    A

**5.** Jones still invented many things __.__          (T)    A

**6.** What did he invent __?__          T    (A)

# Apply

Use what you know and page 17 to write your own sentences that tell. Answer each question with a telling sentence. Remember to start your sentences with a capital letter and end them with a period.

**Answers may vary. Possible answers appear below.**

**7.** When was Frederick Jones born?

_Frederick Jones was born in 1893._

**8.** What kind of work did Frederick Jones do?

_He invented things._

**9.** How did he help truck drivers?

_He invented a way to keep food cold._

**10.** What are two kinds of food that must stay cold?

_Meat and milk must stay cold._

**11.** Some trucks carry food long distances. Why do trucks need to keep this food cold?

_The food will spoil if it does not stay cold._

**12.** Does all food have to stay cold?

_Not all food has to stay cold._

Copyright © Zaner-Bloser, Inc.

# Sentences That Ask

## Learn

a. Do you know about Barbara Jordan?

b. She was the first black woman from the South in Congress.

Which sentence asks you something, **a.** or **b.**? _____ a.

> An **asking sentence** asks a question. It ends with a question mark. A **telling sentence** makes a statement. It ends with a period.

## Practice

If the sentence is a telling sentence, circle **T**. If the sentence is an asking sentence, circle **A**. Write a period (**.**) at the end of each telling sentence. Write a question mark (**?**) at the end of each asking sentence.

1. Barbara Jordan was from Texas ___ .          (T)     A

2. How did she begin her career in politics ___ ?          T     (A)

3. She started by addressing envelopes ___ .          (T)     A

4. One day a speaker did not come ___ .          (T)     A

5. Did she step in for the missing speaker ___ ?          T     (A)

6. Jordan took the speaker's place ___ .          (T)     A

# Apply

Read the paragraph about Barbara Jordan. Then write six questions that are answered in the paragraph.

**Students' questions will vary. Sample questions appear below.**

Barbara Jordan was born in 1939. She died in 1996. She was a great speaker. Her speeches brought people together. She was also the first black woman to do many things. She was the first to be a Texas state senator. She was the first black woman from the South in the U.S. Congress. She did a good job. She was elected again. After that, Jordan went back to Texas. She taught at a college. She also helped the governor of Texas.

7. **When was Barbara Jordan born?**

8. **Was she a great speaker?**

9. **What did her speeches do?**

10. **What job did she have in Texas?**

11. **Why was she elected again in Texas?**

12. **What person did she help in Texas?**

# Telling or Asking Sentences

## Learn

**a.** Do you belong to the Sierra Club?

**b.** It was started by John Muir.

Which sentence tells something, **a.** or **b.**?    __**b.**__

Which sentence asks something, **a.** or **b.**?    __**a.**__

> A **telling sentence** makes a statement. It ends with a period. An **asking sentence** asks a question. It ends with a question mark. Both sentences begin with a capital letter.

## Practice

Write a period at the end of each telling sentence. Write a question mark at the end of each asking sentence.

**1.** John Muir loved nature __.__

**2.** He lived from 1838 until 1914 __.__

**3.** Muir started a special club __.__

**4.** Did you know that he loved to walk __?__

**5.** Once he walked from Indianapolis to the Gulf of Mexico __.__

**6.** Isn't that a long way to walk __?__

# Apply

Rewrite each telling sentence as an asking sentence. Rewrite each asking sentence as a telling sentence. There will usually be more than one way to write each sentence.

**Answers will vary. Possible answers appear below.**

**7.** Muir wanted to protect the wilderness.

Did Muir want to protect the wilderness?

**8.** Did he spend much of his time in California?

He spent much of his time in California.

**9.** Was he also interested in glaciers?

He was also interested in glaciers.

**10.** In 1892, Muir started the Sierra Club.

Did Muir start the Sierra Club in 1892?

**11.** Have many natural sites been named for John Muir?

Many natural sites have been named for John Muir.

**12.** Is John Muir famous for his work with nature?

John Muir is famous for his work with nature.

# Sentences That Command

## Learn

**a.** Paul Revere warned the American colonists about the British.

**b.** Listen to this poem about him.

Which sentence tells the reader what to do, **a.** or **b.**? ___**b.**___

> A **sentence that commands** tells the reader what to do. The first word is often a verb. A sentence that commands ends with a period or an exclamation point. It begins with a capital letter.

## Practice

Circle **T** if the sentence tells something. Circle **A** if it asks something. Circle **C** if it is a command.

**1.** Have you heard of Paul Revere?    T   (A)   C

**2.** Learn about him in your social studies book.    T   A   (C)

**3.** He rode his horse through the countryside.    (T)   A   C

**4.** Keep reading to find out why.    T   A   (C)

**5.** What was Revere shouting?    T   (A)   C

**6.** He was shouting that the British were coming.    (T)   A   C

# Apply

Pretend you are Paul Revere. You need to warn the American colonists that the British soldiers are coming. Rewrite these sentences so they are commands. Your sentences might end with periods or exclamation points.

**Students' sentences may vary. Possible answers appear below.**

**7.** You should tell everyone that the British are coming.

_Tell everyone that the British are coming!_

**8.** You should get ready to fight the British soldiers.

_Get ready to fight the British soldiers!_

**9.** You should warn your friends and neighbors.

_Warn your friends and neighbors!_

**10.** No one should be afraid of the soldiers.

_Don't be afraid of the soldiers._

**11.** Would you please give my horse some water?

_Please give my horse some water._

**12.** Would you tell me the shortest way to the next town?

_Tell me the shortest way to the next town._

*Strategies for Writers—Conventions & Skills Practice*  Unit I

Name _____

# Sentences That Show Strong Feelings

## Learn

**a.** Look at that runner go!

**b.** Is that Jesse Owens?

Which sentence shows strong feelings, **a.** or **b.**?    _a._

> A **sentence that shows strong feelings** usually ends with an exclamation point. It begins with a capital letter.

## Practice

Write a period at the end of each sentence that tells. Write an exclamation point at the end of each sentence that shows strong feelings.

**1.** Jesse Owens was a track star __.__

**2.** What an athlete he was __!__

**3.** He ran in the 1936 Olympic Games in Germany __.__

**4.** Adolf Hitler was the leader of Germany __.__

**5.** He did not think Owens could win __.__

**6.** Hitler was in for a surprise __!__

# Apply

Read these paragraphs about Jesse Owens. Choose six sentences that you think show strong feelings. Write them on the lines. Replace the periods with exclamation points.

Jesse Owens went to The Ohio State University. In 1935, he entered a college track meet. He set three world records. It took him only 45 minutes.

At the 1936 Olympics, Owens won four gold medals. He was the first American to do that. These Olympics were held in Germany. German fans cheered for Owens, too. Hitler was furious. He thought a German runner should win the medals. What a mistake he made.

**Answers will vary. Possible answers appear below.**

7. He set three world records!

8. It took him only 45 minutes!

9. He was the first American to do that!

10. German fans cheered for Owens, too!

11. Hitler was furious!

12. What a mistake he made!

Name _____

# Nouns

## Learn

**Alligators** live **in** swamps.

Which word in dark type names a person, place, or thing?
_____

- - - - - - - - - - - - Alligators - - - - - - - - - - - -
_____
_____

> A **noun** is a word that names a person, place, or thing.

## Practice

Find the two underlined words in each sentence.
Circle the underlined word that is a noun.

**1.** Alligators <u>spend</u> most of their (time) in water.

**2.** They have webbed (feet) so they can swim <u>fast</u>.

**3.** Their strong (tails) push them <u>through</u> the water.

**4.** Half <u>of</u> the (animal) is its tail.

**5.** Alligators <u>hunt</u> for food at (night).

**6.** They have sharp <u>teeth</u> and strong (jaws).

# Apply

Circle each word in the Word Bank that is a noun. Then decide which circled noun best completes each sentence. Write that noun on the line.

## Word Bank

| | | |
|---|---|---|
| are | (teeth) | lost |
| (food) | (people) | (fish) |
| live | eat | (alligator) |
| (water) | about | sharp |

**Answers may vary. Possible responses appear below.**

**7.** Alligators have about 80 _____ **teeth** _____ .

**8.** When a tooth falls out, the _____ **alligator** _____ grows a new one.

**9.** Alligators eat _____ **fish** _____ , birds, turtles, and snakes.

**10.** They swallow their _____ **food** _____ whole.

**11.** They can swim very fast in the _____ **water** _____ .

**12.** They are not friendly to _____ **people** _____ .

Name _____

# Proper Nouns

## Learn

The antelope lives in (Africa) and other **places**.

Circle the word in dark type that names a certain person, place, or thing.

> A **proper noun** names a certain person, place, or thing. Proper nouns begin with a capital letter.

## Practice

Circle the underlined words that are proper nouns.

**1.** Many antelopes live in (Asia). They look like <u>deer</u>.

**2.** No true <u>antelopes</u> live in (North America).

**3.** The <u>goat</u> of the (Rocky Mountains) is a cousin of the antelope.

**4.** Antelopes live on <u>grasslands</u>. About one fourth of the land on (Earth) is grasslands.

**5.** Grasslands look like the (Atlantic Ocean). They are a <u>sea</u> of grass.

**6.** (America) has grassy areas called prairies. Other <u>countries</u> have grasslands, too.

*Strategies for Writers—Conventions & Skills Practice*   Unit 2

# Apply

Choose a proper noun from the Word Bank to complete each sentence. Write the proper noun on the line.

## Word Bank

Isaiah                    Mr. Chow
Africa                    Ms. Ortega
*Animal World*            Columbus Zoo

**Answers may vary. Possible answers appear below.**

**7.** Our class saw four antelopes at the **Columbus Zoo**.

**8.** **Mr. Chow** said that their horns are hollow.

**9.** Antelopes run fast to escape the lions in **Africa**.

**10.** **Ms. Ortega** told us that some antelopes are as small as rabbits.

**11.** I read in the book **Animal World** that antelopes can bounce high in the air.

**12.** My friend **Isaiah** likes to watch shows about animals.

# Common Nouns and Proper Nouns

## Learn

The puffer fish lives in several **oceans,** including
the (Atlantic Ocean)

Circle the word in dark type that names a certain person,
place, or thing.

> A **common noun** names any person, place, or thing.
> A **proper noun** names a certain person, place, or thing.
> A proper noun begins with a capital letter.

## Practice

Read each sentence. Circle a proper noun to
complete each sentence.

**1.** (My uncle/Uncle Henry) told me about the puffer fish.

**2.** He saw this fish once in the (water/Pacific Ocean).

**3.** People in (some places/Japan) eat puffer fish.

**4.** Some in (our country/America) have died from these
poisonous fish.

**5.** On (a TV program/"Nova"), these fish puffed up to twice their size.

**6.** Puffer fish don't live in (my state/Ohio).

# Apply

Choose a noun from the Word Bank to complete each sentence. Write it on the line. Write **P** if you used a proper noun. Write **C** if you used a common noun.

## Word Bank

| | |
|---|---|
| cooks | poison |
| Nova | fish |
| Rising Sun Diner | Japan |

**7.** Puffer fish swell up to scare away bigger _____ **fish** **C** _____.

**8.** Puffer fish have a dangerous _____ **poison** **C** _____ in them.

**9.** I learned on _____ **"Nova"** **P** _____ that the poison could kill you.

**10.** This fish must be cooked by special _____ **cooks** **C** _____.

**11.** Many of these cooks live in _____ **Japan** **P** _____.

**12.** My favorite restaurant is _____ **Rising Sun Diner** **P** _____.

# Singular and Plural Nouns

## Learn

[Grasshoppers] are one kind of (insect).

Circle the word in dark type that names one person, place, or thing.

Draw a box around the word in dark type that names two or more people, places, or things.

> A **singular noun** names one person, place, or thing. A **plural noun** names more than one person, place, or thing. Many plural nouns are formed by adding *-s* to the end of the singular noun.

## Practice

Find the underlined noun in each sentence. Circle **S** if the noun is singular. Circle **P** if the noun is plural.

1. The <u>book</u> says grasshoppers hop, walk, and fly.   Ⓢ   P

2. Grasshoppers can make a noise with their <u>legs</u>.   S   Ⓟ

3. Grasshoppers live in <u>places</u> with tall grass.   S   Ⓟ

4. Most birds eat bugs, even the <u>grasshopper</u>.   Ⓢ   P

5. The grasshopper's color helps it hide from <u>birds</u>.   S   Ⓟ

6. There are many kinds of bugs in our <u>garden</u>.   Ⓢ   P

## Apply

Choose a noun from the Word Bank to complete each sentence. Write it on the line. Write **S** if the noun is singular. Write **P** if the noun is plural.

### Word Bank

| | | |
|---|---|---|
| wings | legs | plants |
| egg | head | holes |

**7.** A grasshopper has a ___**head**   **S**___, two wings, and six legs.

**8.** They breathe through ___**holes**   **P**___ in their bodies.

**9.** They hop with their back ___**legs**   **P**___.

**10.** A grasshopper hatches from an ___**egg**   **S**___.

**11.** A young grasshopper has no ___**wings**   **P**___.

**12.** Most of these bugs eat only ___**plants**   **P**___.

*Strategies for Writers—Conventions & Skills Practice*  **Unit 2**          Copyright © Zaner-Bloser, Inc.

# Action Verbs

## Learn

Owls **hunt** for small animals at **night**.

Write the word in dark type that tells what owls do. _____**hunt**_____

> An **action verb** tells what the subject does or did.

## Practice

Each sentence has two underlined words. Circle the word that is an action verb.

**1.** Owls (eat) mice, insects, frogs, and birds.

**2.** Owls (hunt) these animals in the dark.

**3.** The owls (listen) for sounds from the animals, too.

**4.** Then the owls (fly) very quietly to the animals.

**5.** They (grab) the animals with their strong claws.

**6.** Most owls (sleep) during the day.

# Apply

Circle each word in the Word Bank that is an action verb. Then decide which circled verb best completes each sentence. Write that verb on the line.

## Word Bank

owls     teeth     (tear)

animals     (swallow)     food

(live)     (borrow)     (turn)

chunks     (see)

7. Owls **swallow** small animals whole.

8. They **tear** bigger animals into chunks.

9. To look around, owls **turn** their heads completely around.

10. Owls **see** things in black and white, not color.

II. Different kinds of owls **live** in many different places.

12. They even **borrow** the nests of other birds for themselves.

# Verbs That Tell About the Past

## Learn

The dodo bird (lived) in rain **forests** long ago.

Circle the word in dark type that shows the action happened in the past.

> **Past tense verbs** show that an action happened in the past. Many past tense verbs end with *-ed.*

## Practice

These sentences tell about things that happened in the past. Circle each underlined word that is in the past tense.

**1.** The dodo bird (looked) a little strange.

**2.** It (weighed) about 50 pounds.

**3.** Its short, stubby wings (stopped) it from flying.

**4.** It (walked) on the ground and ate fruit.

**5.** People (hunted) and (cooked) the dodo bird.

**6.** These birds all (died) a long time ago.

# Apply

Choose a word from the Word Bank that best completes each sentence. Complete each sentence by writing the past tense form of the verb on the line.

## Word Bank

| help | disappear | vanish |
| call | stay | pick |

**Answers may vary. Possible responses appear below.**

**7.** The dodo bird _____**stayed**_____ on an island near Africa.

**8.** It _____**picked**_____ the fruit of only one kind of tree.

**9.** People _____**called**_____ that tree the "dodo tree."

**10.** The last dodo _____**vanished**_____ in 1681.

**11.** No one _____**helped**_____ it to survive.

**12.** The dodo _____**disappeared**_____ forever.

*Strategies for Writers—Conventions & Skills Practice* **Unit 2**

Name _____

# Noun or Verb

## Learn

Polar **bears** like snow.

Is the word in dark type used as a noun or verb? _____**a noun**_____

> Some words can be used as **nouns** or as **verbs**. For example *leaves*, can be a noun meaning "parts of a plant" or a verb meaning "goes away." You must read the sentence to tell what the meaning is.

## Practice

Find the underlined word in each sentence. Circle **N** if the word is a noun. Circle **V** if the word is a verb.

**1.** A polar <u>bear</u> has very thick fur.                          (N)    V

**2.** When seals see the bears, they <u>head</u> for the water.      N    (V)

**3.** The bears <u>catch</u> seals in the water.                      N    (V)

**4.** Their <u>hunt</u> for food can take the bears miles from land.  (N)    V

**5.** In the water, the bears <u>paddle</u> with their front feet.    N    (V)

**6.** Polar bears can <u>run</u> very fast.                           N    (V)

Find the underlined word in each sentence. Write **N** on the line if the word is being used as a noun. Write **V** on the line if it is being used as a verb. If the word is a noun, write a sentence using it as a verb. If the word is a verb, write a sentence using it as a noun.

**Answers will vary.**

**7.** Polar bears do not <u>drink</u> water.

V _____

_____

**8.** They do not mind a <u>swim</u> in the icy ocean.

N _____

_____

**9.** They are also not bothered by the bitter <u>wind</u>.

N _____

_____

**10.** When it <u>snows</u>, the seals cannot see the white bears.

V _____

_____

**11.** Polar bears <u>grip</u> the snow with their feet.

V _____

_____

**12.** Baby bears play outside in the <u>spring</u>.

N _____

_____

Name _____

# Adjectives That Tell How Many

## Learn

Newts are **brightly** colored and about **four** inches long.

Which word in dark type tells how many? ____four____

---

An **adjective** tells about a noun. Some adjectives tell how many. They include words such as *three, nine, twelve, few, many,* and *some.*

---

## Practice

Two words are underlined in each sentence. Circle the adjective that tells how many. Put a box around the noun it tells about.

**1.** Newts and frogs are (two) kinds of amphibians.

**2.** Newts live in (three) places: North America, Europe, and Asia.

**3.** Newts have (four) fingers on each front leg.

**4.** They have (five) toes on each back leg.

**5.** Some newts change color when they are about (three) years old.

**6.** Most newts are less than (six) inches long.

# Apply

Read each sentence. Write the adjective from the
Word Bank that best completes each sentence on the line.
Then underline the noun that each adjective tells about.
(You will not use all the words in the Word Bank.)

## Word Bank

| | | |
|---|---|---|
| one | two | three |
| seven | four | five |
| six | few | many |

**Answers may vary. Possible responses appear below.**

**7.** Jason has two frogs, two toads, and a newt. He has _____ **five** _____ pets.

**8.** Jason's newt is covered with _____ **many** _____ spots.

**9.** _____ **One** _____ kind of newt stays in water. The other goes on land.

**10.** Like frogs and toads, all newts have _____ **four** _____ legs.

**11.** All _____ **three** _____ kinds of amphibians lay their eggs in water.

**12.** Jason asked for a dog and a cat. His mom said that

_____ **seven** _____ animals are too many.

*Strategies for Writers—Conventions & Skills Practice* **Unit 2**    Copyright © Zaner-Bloser, Inc.

Name _____

# Other Adjectives

## Learn

Raccoons have **black** patches around their **eyes**.

Which word in dark type tells about a noun?    **black**

Which noun does this word tell about?    **patches**

An **adjective** tells about a noun. Adjectives make sentences more interesting.

## Practice

In each sentence, find an adjective that tells about a noun. Circle the adjective and the noun it tells about.

**I.** Raccoons live in (many places).

**2.** Some live in (dark forests).

**3.** (Busy towns) also have raccoons.

**4.** Raccoons eat (small animals), such as frogs, birds, and mice.

**5.** They have (dark rings) around their eyes.

**6.** Raccoons also have (bushy tails).

# Apply

Write an adjective from the Word Bank to best complete each sentence. Then underline the noun in the sentence that the adjective tells about.

## Word Bank

| | | |
|---|---|---|
| important | funny | sneaky |
| other | enough | different |

**Answers may vary. Possible answers appear below.**

7. Raccoons can live in many _____**different**_____ places.

8. They can find _____**enough**_____ food almost anywhere.

9. These _____**important**_____ skills help them survive.

10. Raccoons hunt at night, while most _____**other**_____ animals sleep.

11. Their face masks make them look like _____**sneaky**_____ robbers.

12. There are many _____**funny**_____ stories about raccoons.

# And, Or, But

## Learn

Many crabs **eat** plants **and** animals.

Circle the word in dark type that joins two other words.

> The words **and, or**, and **but** can join two words in a sentence. They can also join two short sentences.

## Practice

Read each sentence. Circle the words that join two other words or two short sentences.

**1.** Crabs have eight legs **and** two claws.

**2.** Crabs do not have a backbone, **but** most have a shell.

**3.** Hermit crabs do not have a backbone **or** a hard shell.

**4.** Crabs can live on land **or** in the ocean.

**5.** Crabs in the ocean have gills, **but** land crabs do not.

**6.** Some crabs are tiny, **but** other crabs are huge.

# Apply

Add **and**, **or**, or **but** to complete each sentence.
For some sentences, two of these words may make sense.

**Answers may vary. Possible responses appear below.**

**7.** There are two groups of crabs. They are true crabs __**and**__

hermit crabs.

**8.** Hermit crabs steal old shells __**and**__ live in them.

**9.** Crabs can walk __**and/or**__ run sideways.

**10.** Most crabs are small, __**but**__ the Japanese spider crab

can grow 12 feet wide.

**11.** Crabs' eyes stick out from their heads, __**but**__ they can

still see well.

**12.** People boil __**or/and**__ fry crabs to eat.

Name _____

# *Its* and *It's*

## Learn

Earth **is** a big place. Most of (**its**) surface is water.

Circle the word in dark type that means "belonging to it".

> **Its** means "belonging to it." *Its* is often confused with *it's*. *It's* is a contraction of "it is."

## Practice

Read the sentences below. Circle **its** or **it's** to complete each sentence correctly.

**1.** Earth has seven continents on (its/it's) surface.

**2.** The land has (its/it's) mountains, valleys, and plains.

**3.** The planet has many areas. Some of (its/it's) areas are crowded.

**4.** A desert has few people because of (its/it's) poor soil.

**5.** Few people live on a mountain. (Its/It's) soil is too rocky to farm.

**6.** People like to live on a plain. (Its/It's) surface is good for crops.

# Apply

The word **its** will fit once in each sentence below. Cross out the words you are replacing and rewrite the sentences using **its**. The first one is done for you.

**Answers may vary. Possible answers appear below.**

**7.** Many crops can grow on ~~a plain's~~ rich soil.

**Many crops can grow on its rich soil.**

**8.** ~~A valley's~~ soil is rich and deep.

**Its soil is rich and deep.**

**9.** Some people live in a rocky area because of ~~the area's~~ minerals.

**Some people live in a rocky area because of its minerals.**

**10.** Some people on Earth live on ~~Earth's~~ islands.

**Some people on Earth live on its islands.**

**11.** We cannot live without water because we need ~~water's~~ help.

**We cannot live without water because we need its help.**

**12.** An ocean is huge. ~~An ocean's~~ beauty is hard to ignore.

**An ocean is huge. Its beauty is hard to ignore.**

Name _____

# *Its* and *It's*

## Learn

Earth has many kinds of land on its surface. It's an amazing place.

Circle the word in dark type that means "it is."
Put a box around the word that means "belonging to it."

> **It's** is a contraction of "it is." *It's* is often confused with *its*. *Its* means "belonging to it."

## Practice

Read the sentences below. Circle **it's** or **its** to complete each sentence correctly.

**1.** A plain is mostly flat. (It's/Its) surface might have forests.

**2.** Most people live on a plain. (It's/Its) a good place to raise crops.

**3.** A plain can have short grass. Then (it's/its) called a steppe.

**4.** A desert is hot and sandy. (It's/Its) very dry.

**5.** A desert has few plants or animals because of (it's/its) dry soil.

**6.** Antarctica is dry and very cold. (It's/Its) a desert, too.

Use **it's** or **its** to complete each sentence. Write the correct form on the line.

**7.** Tundra is another type of land.

_____**It's**\_\_\_\_\_ covered with snow more than half of the year.

**8.** The tundra is cold and dry.

_____**It's**\_\_\_\_\_ a home to only a few people.

**9.** In the spring, small plants cover the tundra.

_____**It's**\_\_\_\_\_ strange to see their bright flowers.

**10.** Much of Earth was once covered with forests.

However, _____**its**\_\_\_\_\_ forests are disappearing.

**11.** The rain forest has very tall trees.

Because of this, _____**it's**\_\_\_\_\_ dark on the ground of the rain forest.

**12.** Learn all you can about Earth and _____**its**\_\_\_\_\_ many kinds of land.

# A and An

## Learn

The ocean is **an** enormous body of water. It is (a) good source of food and minerals.

Circle the word in dark type that comes before a word beginning with a consonant sound.

> A and **an** are special adjectives. They are called **articles**. Use *a* before a word that begins with a consonant sound: **a** banana. Use *an* before a word that begins with a vowel sound: **an** apple.

## Practice

Read the sentences below. Circle **a** or **an** to complete each sentence correctly.

**1.** Without (a/(an)) ocean, there would be no life on Earth.

**2.** The ocean is (a/(an)) interesting place. We are still trying to understand it.

**3.** It has ((a)/an) big influence on our weather.

**4.** The Pacific Ocean covers nearly ((a)/an) third of Earth.

**5.** It covers (a/(an)) area of almost 70 million square miles.

**6.** The Atlantic Ocean is ((a)/an) body of water off the east coast of the United States.

Circle **a** or **an** in each sentence. If the word is used correctly, write **Correct**. If it is not used correctly, write **a** or **an** on the line to finish the sentence correctly.

**7.** (An) little of Earth's water is in lakes and rivers. Most of the water on Earth is in the oceans.

_____ A _____

**8.** Have you ever visited (a) ocean?

_____ an _____

**9.** Did you take (a) taste of the water? It's very salty!

_____ Correct _____

**10.** The ocean floor is (an) good source of oil and gas.

_____ a _____

**11.** The energy in tides is (a) important source of electricity.

_____ an _____

**12.** Earth's oceans have (a) great deal to teach us.

_____ Correct _____

# Their and They're

## Learn

Do you know where Earth's highest and lowest places are?
**They're** in Asia.

Circle whether the word in dark type means
"belonging to them" or ("they are.")

> The words **their** and **they're** have different spellings
> and different meanings. *Their* means "belonging to
> them." *They're* is a contraction of "they are."

## Practice

Read each sentence below. Circle **their** or **they're** to
complete each sentence correctly.

**1.** Africa and Asia are big. (Their/They're) climates are different.

**2.** Where do most of Earth's people live? (Their/They're) living in Asia.

**3.** One Asian country has a billion people. (Their/They're) in China.

**4.** The people of Asia differ in (their/they're) customs.

**5.** People lived in Asia long ago. (Their/They're) the first to live in cities.

**6.** Other countries put (their/they're) own leaders in charge in Asia.

# Apply

Find the underlined words in each sentence. Cross them out and rewrite the sentence using **their** or **they're** correctly.

**7.** Now most Asian countries have ~~the countries'~~ own rulers.

Now most Asian countries have their own rulers.

**8.** ~~The countries are~~ trying to improve the way people live.

They're trying to improve the way people live.

**9.** Sometimes nations disagree over ~~the nations'~~ borders.

Sometimes nations disagree over their borders.

**10.** Wars between nations add to ~~the nations'~~ problems.

Wars between nations add to their problems.

**11.** Europe and Asia are next to each other. ~~These two areas are~~ sometimes called Eurasia.

They're sometimes called Eurasia.

**12.** Many different people make ~~the peoples'~~ homes in Eurasia.

Many different people make their homes in Eurasia.

*Strategies for Writers—Conventions & Skills Practice*  Unit 3

# They're and There

## Learn

Africa is the second largest continent. Sudan is the largest country **there**.

Circle whether the word in dark type means "they are" or ⟨"in that place."⟩

> The words **they're** and **there** have different spellings and different meanings. *They're* is a contraction of "they are." *There* means "at or in that place."

## Practice

Read each sentence below. Circle **they're** or **there** to complete each sentence correctly.

**1.** Part of Africa is a rain forest. Tall trees grow (⟨there⟩/they're).

**2.** Parts of Africa are another kind of land. (There/⟨They're⟩) called grasslands.

**3.** The world's largest desert is also (they're/⟨there⟩). It is the Sahara.

**4.** Africa has diamonds and gold. (There/⟨They're⟩) found deep in mines.

**5.** Africa's soil is thin and poor. Crops do not grow well (⟨there⟩/they're).

**6.** Africa has some interesting animals. Lions, elephants, and giraffes live (⟨there⟩/they're).

# Apply

Find the underlined words in each sentence. Cross them out and rewrite each sentence using **they're** or **there** correctly.

**7.** Many African people live in small villages. ~~These Africans are~~ farmers.

**They're farmers.**

**8.** They live like people did long ago. On many farms ~~in Africa,~~ life is hard.

**On many farms there, life is hard.**

**9.** Many African nations need help. ~~These nations are~~ working to feed their people.

**They're working to feed their people.**

**10.** Many Africans move to cities. Jobs are easier to find ~~in those places~~.

**Jobs are easier to find there.**

**11.** Africans live longer now. The population ~~in that area~~ is growing.

**The population there is growing.**

**12.** Many Africans come to the United States to study. ~~Some African students are~~ becoming doctors and returning to Africa to work.

**They're becoming doctors and returning to Africa to work.**

# Their, There, and They're

## Learn

Many Americans cannot name the third largest continent. Still, **they're** living on it.

Circle whether the word in dark type means "belonging to them," "in that place," or ("they are.")

> The words **their, there,** and **they're** have different spellings and different meanings. *Their* means "belonging to them." *There* means "at or in that place." *They're* is a contraction of "they are."

## Practice

Read each sentence below. Circle **their, there,** or **they're** to complete each sentence correctly.

**1.** (Their/(There)/They're) are three oceans that border North America.

**2.** North American coasts are known for ((their)/there/they're) beaches.

**3.** How is the climate (their/(there)/they're)?

**4.** Mexico is great! Have you been (their/(there)/they're)?

**5.** Central American countries are small. (Their/There/(They're)) part of North America, too.

**6.** Canada is part of North America. (Their/(There)/They're) are interesting places to visit there.

# Apply

You live in North America, so you can answer these questions. Write a sentence to answer each question. Use **their, there,** or **they're** correctly in your answer.

**Answers may vary. Possible answers appear below.**

**7.** Which ocean is on the west coast? Is it the Pacific or the Atlantic?

**The Pacific Ocean is there.**

**8.** What big mountains go from Alaska to Mexico?

**They're called the Rocky Mountains.**

**9.** Name two countries in North America that share their border.

**Mexico and the United States share their border.**

**10.** Where are the Great Lakes?

**They're between the United States and Canada.**

**11.** Where would you like to go in North America? Why?

**I would like to go to Canada and see a moose there.**

**12.** Can you name the Great Lakes?

**Their names are Erie, Superior, Michigan, Huron, and Ontario.**

*Strategies for Writers—Conventions & Skills Practice* **Unit 3**

# The Verb Go

## Learn

Our teacher has (gone) all over the world. She **went** to South America last year.

Circle the verb in dark type that is used with the word *has*.

> Do not add *-ed* to **go** to make the past tense. It has different forms. The past tense of *go* is *went*: I *went* to school yesterday. Use *gone* with *have, has,* or *had*: They *have gone* to school.

## Practice

Read each sentence below. Circle **go, went,** or **gone** to complete each sentence correctly.

**1.** Have you ever (went/(gone)) to South America?

**2.** Our teacher (go/(went)) there last year.

**3.** Many people live in the cities there. The population has (go/(gone)) up quickly.

**4.** People from farms ((go)/gone) to the cities to find jobs.

**5.** They do not make much money. Some ((go)/gone) back to their farms.

**6.** For other people, things have (went/(gone)) much better. They stay in the cities.

Circle the form of the verb **go** in each sentence. If the verb is correct, write **Correct** on the line. If the verb is not correct, write the correct form. It might be **go, went,** or **gone**.

**7.** The Andes Mountains (gone) along the west coast of South America.

_____ **go** _____

**8.** They are the longest mountain range on Earth. They (went) from Venezuela to the tip of South America.

_____ **go** _____

**9.** Have you ever (went) up a mountain?

_____ **gone** _____

**10.** In the lower mountains, you will find grassy fields. If you (go) higher, you will find snow.

_____ **Correct** _____

**11.** My teacher (gone) on a hike into the mountains.

_____ **went** _____

**12.** If you (go) hiking, make sure you bring plenty of water to drink.

_____ **Correct** _____

*Strategies for Writers—Conventions & Skills Practice*  **Unit 3**

# The Verb *Eat*

## Learn

Australia is both a continent and a country. People there (**eat**) a lot of meat. After they have **ate** a meal, they often drink tea.

Circle the word in dark type that is used correctly.

> Do not add *-ed* to **eat** to make the past tense. It has different forms. The past tense of *eat* is *ate:* I *ate* an apple. Use *eaten* with *have, has,* or *had:* He *has eaten* two apples.

## Practice

Read each sentence below. Circle **eat, ate,** or **eaten** to complete each sentence correctly.

1. Australians raise cattle. The animals (eat/eaten) grass in the fields.

2. Thousands of rabbits in Australia had (ate/eaten) the crops and grass.

3. Kangaroos and other wild animals also (eat/eaten) the grass.

4. Koalas have never (eat/eaten) grass. They only like the leaf of one tree.

5. My aunt (ate/eaten) at several restaurants in Australia.

6. The weather there is sunny and warm. People (eat/eaten) outside all year.

Circle the form of the verb **eat** in each sentence. If the verb is correct, write **Correct** on the line. If the verb is not correct, write the correct form. It might be **eat, ate,** or **eaten.**

**7.** Australians like beef, lamb, chicken, and pork. Have you (ate) these kinds of meat?

_____
**eaten**
_____

**8.** Many Australians (eaten) mild food. They do not like spicy food.

_____
**eat**
_____

**9.** Some Australians (eat) only vegetables. They don't like meat.

_____
**Correct**
_____

**10.** My aunt (eat) Chinese food when she was in Australia.

_____
**ate**
_____

**11.** Many cooks in Australia come from other countries. Australians have (eaten) many kinds of food.

_____
**Correct**
_____

**12.** After they have (ate) they like to drink a cup of tea.

_____
**eaten**
_____

# The Verb *Come*

## Learn

Europe is a small continent with many people. Many Europeans have (come) to the United States.  Maybe they **came** here to escape the crowds!

Circle the verb in dark type that is used with the word *have*.

> Do not add -*ed* to **come** to make the past tense. It has different forms. The past tense of *come* is *came:* She *came* to school late. Use *come* with *have, has,* or *had:* She *has* never *come* late before.

## Practice

Read the sentences below. Circle **come** or **came** to complete each sentence correctly.

**1.** My grandmother (come/came) from Russia. Part of Russia is in Europe.

**2.** Her friends have (come/came) to our house to visit.

**3.** Not many people (come/came) to America from Vatican City. It is the smallest country in Europe.

**4.** The first people to live in Europe probably (come/came) from Asia.

**5.** Some had (come/came) from northern Africa.

**6.** People have (come/came) to the United States from all over the world.

# Apply

Circle the form of the verb **come** in each sentence. If the verb is correct, write **Correct** on the line. If the verb is not correct, write the correct form. It might be **come** or **came**.    Answers may vary. Possible answers appear below.

**7.** Europeans have (came) from many parts of the world.

— — — — — — — — — — come; have come — — — — — — — — — —

**8.** World wars were fought in Europe. Soldiers (come) to Europe from all over the world.

— — — — — — — — — — came — — — — — — — — — —

**9.** Where did your family (came) from?

— — — — — — — — — — come — — — — — — — — — —

**10.** Many visitors to Europe have (came) from the United States.

— — — — — — — — — — come; have come — — — — — — — — — —

**11.** Today, many visitors to the United States (come) from Europe.

— — — — — — — — — — Correct; have come — — — — — — — — — —

**12.** My grandmother (come) to my class once to speak about Russia.

— — — — — — — — — — came — — — — — — — — — —

# The Verb *Give*

## Learn

Antarctica **gives** us more than ice and snow.
It has (given) us much to learn.

Circle the verb in dark type that is used with the word *has*.

> Do not add -*ed* to **give** to make the past tense. It has different forms. The past tense of *give* is *gave:* He *gave* me a pencil. Use *given* with *have, has,* or *had:* He *had given* me some paper.

## Practice

Read the sentences below. Circle **give, gave,** or **given** to complete each sentence.

**1.** Only people who study Antarctica live there. This place has not (give/given) a home to any other people.

**2.** In 1820, Antarctica (gave/given) explorers a surprise. That's when they saw this continent for the first time.

**3.** Antarctica has many minerals. It is too hard to dig them out. Many companies have (gave/given) up on the task.

**4.** Antarctica's icy winds (give/given) the word *cold* a new meaning.

**5.** However, the cold winds don't (give/gave) this land any rain. It hardly ever even snows!

**6.** Have you ever (give/given) thought to reading more about this place?

Circle the form of the verb **give** in each sentence. If the verb is correct, write **Correct** on the line. If the verb is not correct, write the correct form. It might be **give** or **gives, gave,** or **given**.

**7.** Every summer, Antarctica give off huge icebergs.

_gives_

**8.** Icebergs given people on ships a scare. Icebergs can be 5,000 square miles.

_give_

**9.** The Antarctic ice cap is huge. Its thickest spot is given as 15,700 feet.

**Correct**

**10.** My uncle once give some thought to going down there.

_gave_

**11.** The cold has gave this continent a bad name. I think it is an interesting place.

_given_

**12.** Not many people given their time to studying this harsh land.

_give_

*Strategies for Writers—Conventions & Skills Practice*  **Unit 3**

Name _____

# Making the Subject and Verb Agree

## Learn

This (story) tells about the three little pigs. The **pigs** build three houses.

Circle the subject in dark type that tells about one thing (singular). Draw a line under the subject in dark type that tells about more than one thing (plural).

> The **subject** and its **verb** must **agree**. They must both be singular or both be plural. Add *-s* or *-es* to make the verb singular when the subject is singular. Do not add *-s* or *-es* to the verb when the subject is plural.

## Practice

Read each sentence. Draw a line under the subject of each sentence. Circle the verb that agrees with that subject.

**1.** Two pigs (build/builds) their houses of straw and sticks.

**2.** One pig (build/builds) his house of bricks.

**3.** The big bad wolf (blow/blows) down the first two houses.

**4.** Then he (come/comes) to the house of bricks.

**5.** The wolf (huff/huffs) for a long time.

**6.** The pigs (laugh/laughs) at the wolf.

***Strategies for Writers*—Conventions & Skills Practice   Unit 4**    **67**

# Apply

Choose the verb from the Word Bank that agrees with the subject in each sentence. Write the verb on the line. You will use each verb once.

## Word Bank

| | |
|---|---|
| tell | arrives |
| arrive | tells |
| grows | grow |

7. Then the wolf _____ **tells** _____ the pigs about some apples.

8. The apples _____ **grow** _____ on a tree in an orchard.

9. The pigs _____ **tell** _____ the wolf to meet them at the tree.

10. They _____ **arrive** _____ at the tree before the wolf.

11. He _____ **arrives** _____ too late to grab the pigs.

12. The wolf _____ **grows** _____ very angry!

**Lesson 32**

# More Practice in Making Subjects and Verbs Agree

## Learn

The ducklings **swim** in a row. One duckling (look) different.

Draw a line under the verb in dark type that agrees with its subject. Circle the verb in dark type that does not agree with its subject.

> Remember: the **subject** and its **verb** must **agree**. Add -s or -es to the verb when the subject is singular. Do not add -s or -es when the subject is plural.

## Practice

Read each sentence. Circle the form of the verb that completes each sentence correctly.

1. One duckling _____ last.                          hatch    (hatches)

2. The other ducks _____ fun of him.        (make)    makes

3. They _____ him mean names.                 (call)    calls

4. Mother duck _____ him anyway.            love    (loves)

5. This duckling _____ bigger than the others.    grow    (grows)

6. They _____ him away.                             (chase)    chases

*Strategies for Writers*—Conventions & Skills Practice   Unit 4

# Apply

Choose the verb from the Word Bank that agrees with the subject in each sentence. Write the verb on the line. You will not use all the verbs.

**Answers may vary. Possible answers appear below.**

## Word Bank

| | | |
|---|---|---|
| look | sees | feel |
| thinks | run | change |
| feels | runs | see |
| changes | looks | think |

**7.** The ugly duckling _____ **feels** _____ sad and lonely.

**8.** He _____ **runs** _____ away from his home on the farm.

**9.** Some wild geese _____ **see** _____ the duckling.

**10.** They _____ **think** _____ he is ugly, too.

**11.** As he grows, the duckling _____ **changes** _____.

**12.** The ugly duckling _____ **looks** _____ beautiful now!

*Strategies for Writers—Conventions & Skills Practice* **Unit 4**

# Forms of the Verb *Be*

## Learn

The lion (**was**) asleep. His eyes **were** closed.

Circle the verb in dark type that is used with a singular subject. Draw a line under the verb in dark type that is used with a plural subject.

> Use *is* or *was* with a **singular subject**. Use *are* or *were* with a **plural subject**.

## Practice

Find the underlined subject in each sentence. Circle **S** if the subject is singular. Circle **P** if it is plural. Circle the correct verb for each subject.

1. The <u>mouse</u> ((was)/were) scared of the lion.  (S)  P

2. His <u>paws</u> (was/(were)) bigger than the mouse.  S  (P)

3. A <u>mouse</u> ((is)/are) much smaller than a lion.  (S)  P

4. The <u>lion</u> ((was)/were) angry at the mouse.  (S)  P

5. The <u>mouse</u> ((was)/were) begging for her life.  (S)  P

6. <u>Lions</u> (is/(are)) kind, so he let her go.  S  (P)

# Apply

Draw a line under the form of the verb **be** in each sentence. Choose the subject from the Word Bank that agrees with this verb. Write the subject on the line. You will not use all the words in the Word Bank. Remember to begin each sentence with a capital letter.

**Answers may vary. Possible answers appear below.**

## Word Bank

| | | | |
|---|---|---|---|
| lion | mouse | mice | holes |
| foot | lions | feet | they |
| she | hole | he | paws |

**7.** A few days later, the _____ **lion** _____ <u>was</u> caught in a hunter's net.

**8.** His _____ **feet** _____ <u>were</u> trapped in the net.

**9.** The little _____ **mouse** _____ <u>was</u> walking nearby.

**10.** _____ **Mice** _____ <u>are</u> good at chewing nets.

**11.** Soon a large _____ **hole** _____ <u>was</u> cut in the net.

**12.** The lion was free again! _____ **He** _____ <u>was</u> happy!

Name _____

# Verbs That Tell About the Past

## Learn

Cinderella **mops** the floor. She (**mopped**) it yesterday, too.

Circle the verb in dark type that tells about something that happened in the past.

> The **tense** of a verb shows when an action happens. If the verb is in **present tense,** the action is happening now. If the verb is in **past tense,** the action happened in the past. Many past tense verbs end in *-ed*.

## Practice

Read each sentence. Circle the verb that correctly completes each sentence.

**1.** Cinderella _____ with her stepmother and stepsisters.   **live**   (**lived**)

**2.** She _____ very hard all day long.   **work**  (**worked**)

**3.** Cinderella _____ to the mice in her bedroom.   **talk**   (**talked**)

**4.** She _____ to go to a special dance.   **want**  (**wanted**)

**5.** However, Cinderella _____ a fancy dress.   **need**  (**needed**)

**6.** Then, her fairy godmother _____.   **help**  (**helped**)

# Apply

Choose a verb from the Word Bank to complete each sentence correctly. Write the past tense of the verb on the line. You will use each verb once.

## Word Bank

| turn | whisper | wish |
|------|---------|------|
| smile | wave | ask |

**Answers may vary. Possible answers appear below.**

7. "Why are you here?" Cinderella _____**asked**_____ .

8. "You _____**wished**_____ for a new dress," her godmother said.

9. Then the godmother _____**waved**_____ her wand.

10. Cinderella's rags _____**turned**_____ into a beautiful dress.

11. Cinderella _____**smiled**_____ when she saw the dress.

12. "This dress is so lovely," she _____**whispered**_____ softly.

*Strategies for Writers—Conventions & Skills Practice*   **Unit 4**          Copyright © Zaner-Bloser, Inc.

Name _____

# Choosing the Correct Verb Tense

## Learn

I **listened** to the story, and I **decided** something. Everyone **needs** a fairy godmother.

Circle the verb in dark type that tells about something that is happening right now.

> The **tense** of a verb shows when an action happens. If the action is happening now, the verb is in the **present tense**. If the action happened in the past, the verb is in the **past tense**. Many past tense verbs end in *-ed*.

## Practice

Read each sentence. The verb in each sentence is underlined. Circle **PA** if the verb is in the past tense. Circle **PR** if the verb is in the present tense.

1. Kim <u>loves</u> this part of the story.     PA    (PR)

2. She <u>pretends</u> that she is Cinderella.     PA    (PR)

3. The godmother <u>turned</u> a pumpkin into a coach.     (PA)    PR

4. Next, she <u>touched</u> six mice with her wand.     (PA)    PR

5. Six white horses <u>appeared</u>.     (PA)    PR

6. This part always <u>makes</u> Kim smile.     PA    (PR)

Read each sentence. If the underlined verb is in the present tense, write **PR** on the line. Write the sentence so the verb is in the past tense. If the underlined verb is in the past tense, write **PA** on the line. Write the sentence so the verb is in the present tense. The first one is done for you.

**7.** The six horses <u>pull</u> Cinderella's coach.

**PR**     **The six horses pulled Cinderella's coach.**

**8.** Everyone <u>stops</u> dancing when they saw her.

**PR**     **Everyone stopped dancing when they saw her.**

**9.** The prince <u>dances</u> with Cinderella.

**PR**     **The prince danced with Cinderella.**

**10.** At midnight, Cinderella <u>races</u> home.

**PR**     **At midnight, Cinderella raced home.**

**11.** Kim <u>liked</u> the ending of the story best.

**PA**     **Kim likes the ending of the story.**

**12.** The prince <u>searches</u> his kingdom for Cinderella.

**PR**     **The prince searched his kingdom for Cinderella.**

Name _____

# Subject Pronouns

## Learn

The <u>hare</u> bragged to the other animals. (He) told **them** many stories.

Circle the pronoun in dark type that is the subject of the sentence. Underline the noun that this pronoun replaces.

> A **subject pronoun** takes the place of one or more nouns. *I, you, he, she, it, we,* and *they* are subject pronouns.

## Practice

Read each sentence. Underline the six subject pronouns below. Circle the noun each subject pronoun replaces.

**1.** The hare has one friend, the (crow.) <u>She</u> puts up with him.

**2.** The (hare) loves attention. <u>He</u> talks a lot about himself.

**3.** (People) get tired of the hare's bragging. <u>They</u> leave.

**4.** The hare bragged to his (family) too. <u>They</u> tried to listen and be polite.

**5.** The (tortoise) has no trouble making friends. <u>He</u> is a lot of fun.

**6.** Our whole (class) likes this story. <u>We</u> think it's very funny.

*Strategies for Writers—Conventions & Skills Practice* Unit 4

Read each set of sentences. Choose a pronoun from the Word Bank to complete each sentence correctly. Write the pronoun on the line. You will use all the pronouns. Remember to begin each sentence with a capital letter.

## Word Bank

| I | You | He |
|---|-----|-----|
| They | It | We |

7. The hare said, "Look at my legs, tortoise. _____**They**_____ are much longer than yours."

8. "I challenge you to a race, tortoise. _____**You**_____ will lose!" said the hare.

9. The tortoise was tired of the hare's bragging. _____**He**_____ said, "I will race you."

10. The other animals said, "_____**We**_____ are behind you, tortoise. We hope you win."

11. That day was very sunny. _____**It**_____ was too hot for a race.

12. The hare started the race. "_____**I**_____ will win for sure," he said.

# Object Pronouns

## Learn

The tortoise looked behind (the tortoise). The hare
was still fast asleep.

Circle the words in dark type which could be replaced
with the pronoun **him**.

> An **object pronoun** takes the place of one or more
> nouns. Object pronouns can come after action verbs.
> They also come after words such as *to, at, for, of,*
> *behind,* and *with. Me, you, him, her, it,* and *them* are
> object pronouns.

## Practice

Read each sentence. Draw a line under the six object
pronouns in these sentences. Be careful—not every
pronoun below is an object pronoun!

1. Our teacher told <u>us</u> the story of the tortoise and the hare.

2. Everyone enjoyed <u>it</u> very much.

3. My aunt gave <u>me</u> a book with this story.

4. I drew a picture of the hare and the tortoise for <u>her</u>.

5. She said the picture looked just like <u>them</u>.

6. I drew the tortoise with spots on <u>him</u>.

# Apply

Read the sentences below. Choose a pronoun from the Word Bank to complete each sentence correctly. Write the pronoun on the line. You will use all the pronouns in the Word Bank. Hint: Use the underlined words to help you.

## Word Bank

| me | him | her |
|----|-----|-----|
| it | them | you |

7. At first, <u>the hare</u> ran very fast. The tortoise was far behind _____ **him** _____.

8. The hare saw <u>Sheila</u> sitting in a tree. He waved to _____ **her** _____.

9. Soon the hare came to a shady <u>tree</u>. He sat down under _____ **it** _____ for a little rest.

10. The tortoise's <u>friends</u> were watching the race. He was hot and tired, but he kept going for _____ **them** _____.

11. "They are cheering for _____ **me** _____," <u>the tortoise</u> said.

12. The hare fell asleep and the tortoise won the race! "<u>Tortoise</u>, we were counting on _____ **you** _____," the animals said.

# Choosing the Correct Pronoun

## Learn

Grasshopper did not think about winter. (**He**) was too busy playing. **Him** just wanted to have fun.

Circle the pronoun in dark type that is used correctly.

> Use *I, we, he, she, you, it,* and *they* as **subjects** of sentences. Use *me, us, him, her,* and *them* as **objects** in sentences. *You* and *it* can also be objects in sentences.

## Practice

Read each sentence. Draw a line under the pronoun that completes each sentence correctly.

**1.** Grasshopper wanted Ant to play with (he/<u>him</u>).

**2.** Ant was gathering seeds. He was storing (they/<u>them</u>) for winter.

**3.** "Please play with (<u>me</u>/I)," Grasshopper said.

**4.** "(Me/<u>I</u>) can't right now," Ant told him. "There is no time."

**5.** (<u>He</u>/Him) kept gathering food for the winter.

**6.** The days got shorter. (<u>They</u>/Them) got colder, too.

*Strategies for Writers*—Conventions & Skills Practice   Unit 4   **81**

# Apply

Read each sentence. Choose a pronoun from the Word Bank to complete each sentence correctly. Write the pronoun on the line. You will not use all the pronouns in the Word Bank. Hint: Use the underlined words to help you.

## Word Bank

| I | We | You | she |
|---|----|-----|-----|
| They | me | us | him |

7. <u>Ant</u> and <u>Grasshopper</u> were neighbors. **They** both needed food when winter came.

8. <u>Ant</u> had plenty of food. Grasshopper asked **him** to share his food.

9. <u>Grasshopper</u> said, "**I** must eat!"

10. Ant said to <u>Grasshopper</u>, "**You** should have planned ahead."

11. Ant said, "<u>Ants</u> are not lazy. **They/We** do not play when there is work to be done."

12. <u>Grasshopper</u> said, "This has been a good lesson for **me**."

Name _____

# Using *I* or *Me* With Another Name

## Learn

Jon and **I** like fairy tales. The teacher asked
Jon and **me** to retell a fairy tale.

Which word in dark type is a subject pronoun? _____**I**_____

> When you talk about yourself, use *I* as a **subject pronoun**. Use *me* as an **object pronoun**. When you talk about yourself and another person, always name the other person first.

## Practice

Read each sentence. Circle **I** or **me** to complete each sentence correctly.

1. Jean and _____ decided to retell "Cinderella."        (I)    me

2. The teacher gave Jean and _____ paper for our story.    I    (me)

3. Then Kevin asked Jean and _____ if he could help us.    I    (me)

4. Jean and _____ were glad to have his help.             (I)    me

5. Kevin wanted to draw the pictures for Jean and _____.   I    (me)

6. Soon Kevin, Jean, and _____ were hard at work.         (I)    me

# Apply

Complete these sentences by writing a name and the pronoun **I** or **me**. You may use the name of a family member, a friend, or someone else. Use the same name in all the sentences. Remember to write the name first.

7. _____**Name**_____ and _____**I**_____ have the same favorite fable.

8. The teacher asked _____**Name**_____ and _____**me**_____ to retell this fable.

9. _____**Name**_____ and _____**I**_____ talked about changes we could make in the fable.

10. Wanda showed _____**Name**_____ and _____**me**_____ the pictures she had drawn for her fable.

11. _____**Name**_____ and _____**I**_____ decided we needed to draw pictures, too.

12. Everyone told _____**Name**_____ and _____**me**_____ that they liked our retold fable.

*Strategies for Writers—Conventions & Skills Practice*  **Unit 4**

Name _____

# Comparing With Adjectives

## Learn

Which is **longer,** a fable or a fairy tale?
Which is the (**longest**) of all?

Circle the adjective in dark type that compares
more than two things.

> An **adjective** can describe by **comparing** two people,
> places, or things. Add *-er* to short adjectives to
> compare two things.
>
> An adjective can also compare more than two people,
> places, or things. Add *-est* to short adjectives to
> compare more than two things.

## Practice

Read each sentence. Draw a line under the correct form
of the adjective in each sentence.

**1.** The lion was much (bigger/biggest) than the mouse.

**2.** He could roar much (louder/loudest) than the mouse.

**3.** Still, the lion was the (kinder/kindest) animal of all in the jungle.

**4.** Cinderella was (kinder/more kind) than her stepsisters.

**5.** She had to do (harder/more hard) work than her sisters.

**6.** Her dress was the (prettier/prettiest) one of all at the dance.

# Apply

Read each sentence. Choose an adjective from the Word Bank that completes each sentence correctly. Write the adjective on the line.

## Word Bank

| | | |
|---|---|---|
| smart | safe | slow |
| strong | slower | smarter |
| slowest | safer | stronger |

**Answers may vary. Possible answers appear below.**

**7.** The tortoise was the _____**slowest**_____ animal of all.

**8.** He was much _____**slower**_____ than the hare.

**9.** However, the tortoise was _____**smarter**_____ than the hare.

**10.** The house of bricks was _____**stronger**_____ than the house of sticks.

**11.** The brick house was the _____**strongest**_____ one of all.

**12.** The pigs were _____**safer**_____ in the brick house than in the stick house.

Name _____

# Capitalizing the
# First Word in a Sentence

## Learn

(our) class likes to draw with crayons, colored pencils, and chalk.

Circle the word in this sentence that should start
with a capital letter.

> Begin every sentence with a **capital letter**.

## Practice

Read the paragraphs below. Find six words that should
begin with a capital letter. Circle the letter that should
be a capital.

(d)o you like to draw? (y)ou can make lines that are straight
or bumpy or jagged. Sometimes our teacher lets us draw with
charcoal. (c)harcoal makes soft, dark lines, but it's kind of messy.
I like to use crayons, too. (i)f you turn a crayon on its side, you can color
a big area. (o)f course, you have to peel the label off the crayon first!
   My friends and I draw pictures for the stories we write.
(t)he pictures help tell the stories. No one minds if our pictures
aren't perfect.

Put each group of words in order to make a sentence.
Write the sentence on the line. Be sure to start it with
a capital letter. Each sentence should end with a period.

**7.** to animals sister draw my likes

My sister likes to draw animals.

**8.** crayons uses markers she and colored

She uses colored markers and crayons.

**9.** start shapes animals out her as

Her animals start out as shapes.

**10.** a might become elephant an circle

A circle might become an elephant.

**11.** a triangle cat become a might

A triangle might become a cat.

**12.** draw shapes with it's to fun

It's fun to draw with shapes.

*Strategies for Writers—Conventions & Skills Practice* Unit 5        Copyright © Zaner-Bloser, Inc.

# Periods and Question Marks

## Learn

**a.** Do you like to paint**?**

**b.** I like watercolors best.

Which sentence, **a.** or **b.**, asks a question? Circle **a.** or **b.**
Circle the end punctuation of this sentence.

> Use a **period** at the end of a telling sentence. Use a
> **question mark** at the end of an asking sentence.

## Practice

Read each sentence. Write the correct end punctuation for
each sentence. It will be a period or a question mark.

**1.** You can paint using a paintbrush or your hands __.__

**2.** I like to feel the paint on my fingers __.__

**3.** Which colors should I mix to make green __?__

**4.** Red and orange are warm colors __.__

**5.** What are some cool colors __?__

**6.** How can you turn black into gray __?__

*Strategies for Writers—Conventions & Skills Practice* Unit 5

Rewrite each telling sentence as an asking sentence. Rewrite each asking sentence as a telling sentence. Be sure to use the correct end punctuation in your new sentences. Remember to start every sentence with a capital letter.

**Answers may vary. Possible answers appear below.**

**7.** Does finger paint take a long time to dry?

**Finger paint takes a long time to dry.**

**8.** It is easy to mix paint colors.

**Is it easy to mix paint colors?**

**9.** Is there too much water in these watercolors?

**There is too much water in these watercolors.**

**10.** Kevin loves to finger paint.

**Does Kevin love to finger paint?**

**11.** Does Anna use dark shades in her painting?

**Anna uses dark shades in her painting.**

**12.** Erin likes painting better than drawing.

**Does Erin like painting better than drawing?**

Copyright © Zaner-Bloser, Inc.

# Periods and Exclamation Points

## Learn

**a.** A sculpture can be made of rock, clay, or wood.

**b.** That sculpture is huge!

Which sentence, **a.** or **b.**, shows strong feelings? Circle **a.** or **b.**

> Use a **period** at the end of a **telling sentence** or a sentence that tells someone to do something (command). Use an **exclamation point** at the end of a sentence that shows strong feelings (exclamation).

## Practice

Circle **T** if the sentence is a telling sentence. Circle **C** if a sentence is a command. Circle **E** if the sentence is an exclamation. Add the correct end punctuation to each sentence.

**Answers may vary. Possible answers appear below.**

**1.** Tell me about your sculpture __.__          T     (C)     E

**2.** I made this sculpture from clay __.__          (T)     C     E

**3.** Your sculpture is amazing __!__          T     C     (E)

**4.** Once I watched someone carve a rock __.__          (T)     C     E

**5.** Look at the details in this sculpture __./!__          T     (C)     (E)

**6.** I never saw so many sculptures before __./!__          (T)     C     (E)

*Strategies for Writers*—Conventions & Skills Practice   Unit 5

# Apply

Pretend you are at a museum with your friends or family. You see an amazing statue. Imagine what it looks like. Then answer these questions. Be sure to use the correct end punctuation.

**Answers may vary. Possible responses appear below.**

**7.** What is the statue made of?

It is made of wood.

**8.** What does the statue look like?

It looks like a little dog.

**9.** What is the most amazing thing about this statue?

It looks so real!

**10.** Tell the people with you to come and see this statue.

Come and see this statue.

**11.** Tell them to look at a certain part of the statue.

Look at his cute ears.

**12.** Explain why you like this statue.

The artist used different kinds of wood.

# Proper Nouns

## Learn

My neighbor is named (carl) He has met some famous **artists**.

Circle the word in dark type that should start with a capital letter.

> **Proper nouns** are the names of particular people, places, or things. Proper nouns begin with a capital letter.

## Practice

Read each sentence. Find the word in dark type in each sentence that is a proper noun and circle its first letter.

**1.** Have you heard of a **painter** named (p)icasso?

**2.** He was born in a **country** called (s)pain.

**3.** He took the last name of his **mother,** (m)aria Picasso.

**4.** When this **man** was older, he moved to (p)aris.

**5.** He studied at the (l)ouvre, which is a **museum**.

**6.** Picasso helped to invent a kind of **painting** called (c)ubism.

# Apply

Find the proper noun in each sentence that should start with a capital letter. Write it correctly on the line.

**7.** Beatrix potter was a writer and an artist.

**Potter**

**8.** She wrote a story about a rabbit named peter.

**Peter**

**9.** She also drew the pictures of peter and his family.

**Peter**

**10.** Potter was born in england in 1866.

**England**

**11.** She spent much of her time with her brother bertram.

**Bertram**

**12.** She often drew a village she loved called sawrey.

**Sawrey**

*Strategies for Writers—Conventions & Skills Practice*   Unit 5

# Abbreviations

## Learn

(Mr.) Thomas read us a story by (Dr.) Seuss.

Circle the two abbreviations in this sentence.

> An **abbreviation** is a short form of a word. It begins with a capital letter and ends with a period. Many **titles of respect,** such as *Mrs.* and *Dr.*, are abbreviations.

## Practice

Read each sentence. Look at the underlined word in each sentence. Circle the correct abbreviation for it.

1. <u>Doctor</u> Seuss's real name is Theodor Geisel.  Mr.  (Dr.)

2. <u>Mister</u> Geisel was both an artist and a writer.  Dr.  (Mr.)

3. He was born in 1904 in Springfield, <u>Massachusetts</u>.  MT  (MA)

4. After studying in England, Geisel returned to the <u>United States</u>.  (U.S.)  U.N.

5. One of his stories is called "And to Think That I Saw It on Mulberry <u>Street</u>."  (St.)  Rd.

6. Geisel died on <u>September</u> 24, 1991.  Set.  (Sept.)

# Apply

Choose an abbreviation from the Word Bank that can be used in place of the underlined word or words. Write the abbreviation for that word or those words on the line.

## Word Bank

| | | |
|---|---|---|
| Mon. | Feb. | D.C. |
| Sat. | Ave. | N.Y. |

**7.** Have you been to the National Gallery of Art in Washington, <u>District of Columbia</u>?

_____ **D.C.** _____

**8.** It is located on Constitution <u>Avenue</u>.

_____ **Ave.** _____

**9.** The gallery's Web site says it's open <u>Monday</u> through Saturday.

_____ **Mon.** _____

**10.** That site has a calendar of what's happening in <u>February</u> or any month.

_____ **Feb.** _____

**11.** Paintings at the gallery can take you on an imaginary trip to <u>New York</u>.

_____ **N.Y.** _____

**12.** Nearly every <u>Saturday</u>, you can watch a film especially for children.

_____ **Sat.** _____

*Strategies for Writers—Conventions & Skills Practice* **Unit 5**

Name _____

**Lesson 46**

# Contractions

## Learn

a.   **We are** going to see a play today.

b.   (We're) taking the bus to the theater.

Look at the words in dark type in sentence **a.**
Circle the word in sentence **b.** that has the same meaning.

> A **contraction** is made up of two words that are put together. Some letters from the two words are left out. An **apostrophe** takes the place of the missing letters.

## Practice

Read each sentence. Circle the contraction that could take the place of the underlined words.

1. I <u>have</u> seen two plays.   I'm   (I've)

2. <u>Did not</u> your class go to a play last week?   (Didn't)   Don't

3. Seeing a play on television <u>is not</u> the same as seeing it on stage.   (isn't)   wasn't

4. <u>Was not</u> the scenery colorful in that play?   Weren't   (Wasn't)

5. <u>You will</u> really like these actors.   You're   (You'll)

6. <u>They are</u> in television shows, too.   (They're)   They've

# Apply

Read each sentence. Find the underlined words in each sentence. Rewrite the sentence making the underlined words a contraction. Remember to begin each sentence with a capital letter.

**7.** <u>She would</u> rather act in a play than paint.

**She'd rather act in a play than paint.**

**8.** <u>She will</u> say her lines loudly.

**She'll say her lines loudly.**

**9.** We <u>cannot</u> find the props.

**We can't find the props.**

**10.** <u>I am</u> confused. Which props do we need?

**I'm confused. Which props do we need?**

**11.** <u>They have</u> recorded a barking dog for Scene 3.

**They've recorded a barking dog for Scene 3.**

**12.** <u>Was not</u> the dog in Scene 2?

**Wasn't the dog in Scene 2?**

*Strategies for Writers—Conventions & Skills Practice*   Unit 5                    Copyright © Zaner-Bloser, Inc.

# Writing Sentences Correctly

## Learn

**a.** do you like to sing?

**b.** My favorite songs are folk music ( **c.** ) I like happy music best.

Circle the letter of the sentence that is written correctly, **a.**, **b.**, or **c.**

> Begin each sentence with a **capital letter**. Put a **period** at the end of a telling sentence and a command. Put a **question mark** at the end of an asking sentence. Put an **exclamation point** at the end of a sentence that shows strong feelings.

## Practice

Circle the letter in each sentence that should be a capital. Write the correct end punctuation for each sentence on the line.

**1.** our music teacher taught us many songs _._

**2.** we clap the beat for some of them _._

**3.** do you know the words for "The Bear Went Over the Mountain" _?_

**4.** please sing "The Wheels on the Bus" with me _._

**5.** We could sing that one forever _!_

**6.** which song is your favorite _?_

Follow the directions for each number below. Make sure your sentences begin with capital letters and end with the correct punctuation.

**Answers will vary. Possible responses appear below.**

**7.** Write a sentence telling the name of your favorite song.

**My favorite song is "This Little Light."**

**8.** Ask someone to sing a song with you.

**Would you sing "Twinkle Twinkle Little Star" with me?**

**9.** Tell something that you really like about singing.

**I like singing loud!**

**10.** Tell the kind of music that a friend or family member likes.

**My brother likes jazz music.**

**11.** Your class is singing a song too softly. Write what your teacher would tell you.

**Please sing louder.**

**12.** Explain how you feel about slow, sad music.

**I don't like it at all!**

# Commas in a Series

## Learn

a. A piano, a flute, and a trumpet all make music.

b. A guitar, a banjo, and a violin are all string instruments.

Circle the commas in sentence **a.**
Add commas where they belong in sentence **b.**

> Use **commas** to separate words in a series. A **series** is
> a list of three or more words.

## Practice

Add commas where they are needed in each sentence.

**1.** My sister, my uncle, and I know how to play the guitar.

**2.** You blow into a harmonica, a whistle, and a kazoo.

**3.** My neighbor plays the drums, piano, and clarinet.

**4.** In that song, I can hear a piano, a flute, and cymbals.

**5.** Is the trumpet, the trombone, or the clarinet your favorite instrument?

**6.** Our marching band has trumpets, drums, and flutes.

*Strategies for Writers—Conventions & Skills Practice* Unit 5

# Apply

Follow the directions for each number below. Be sure to use commas correctly in a series.

**Answers will vary. Possible responses appear below.**

**7.** Write a sentence telling three musical instruments that you would like to play.

__I would like to play the trumpet, cymbals, and guitar.__

**8.** Write a sentence listing three musical instruments with strings.

__Guitars, fiddles, and banjos all have strings.__

**9.** Write a sentence listing three musical instruments that make loud music.

__Drums, trumpets, and cymbals make loud music.__

**10.** Write a sentence listing three instruments that make soft music.

__Pianos, flutes, and guitars can make soft music.__

**11.** Write a sentence naming three people who play an instrument.

__Grandma, Jenna, and Jeff can play musical instruments.__

**12.** Write a sentence naming three places where people play musical instruments.

__People play them at home, at school, and at concerts.__

*Strategies for Writers*—Conventions & Skills Practice   Unit 5     Copyright © Zaner-Bloser, Inc.

# Quotation Marks

## Learn

**a.** "When are we going to the ballet?" Amy asked.

**b.** "We are going there tomorrow," her mother said.

Look at the quotation marks in sentence **a.**
Add quotation marks where they belong in sentence **b.**

> Use **quotation marks** at the beginning and end of a
> speaker's exact words. Use a comma to separate the
> quotation from the rest of the sentence.

## Practice

Add any missing quotation marks in each sentence.

**1.** "Do you like to dance?" Jill asked.

**2.** "I like to square dance," Juan told her.

**3.** "My parents like to square dance," Jill said.

**4.** Jill asked, "Would you go with me to the next square

dance?"

**5.** "I have to ask my parents first," he told her.

**6.** She said, "I hope you can go with me."

Read each sentence. Rewrite each sentence using quotation marks correctly.

**7.** My sister is taking ballet lessons, Jason said.

"My sister is taking ballet lessons," Jason said.

**8.** She must know how to dance on her toes, Tracy said.

"She must know how to dance on her toes," Tracy said.

**9.** Jason answered, No, she isn't old enough to do that.

Jason answered, "No, she isn't old enough to do that."

**10.** He said, she will learn to dance on her toes later.

He said, "She will learn to dance on her toes later."

**11.** I wonder if boys learn to dance on their toes, Tracy said.

"I wonder if boys learn to dance on their toes," Tracy said.

**12.** Jason said, Yes, but they have to be older, too.

Jason said, "Yes, but they have to be older, too."

*Strategies for Writers—Conventions & Skills Practice*  **Unit 5**     Copyright © Zaner-Bloser, Inc.

Name _____

# Book Titles

## Learn

Have you read the book titled <u>my crayons talk</u>?

Draw a line under the title of the book. Circle the three letters in the title that should be capitals.

> **Capitalize** the first word, last word, and all important words in the **title** of a book. **Underline** the book title.

## Practice

Draw a line under the book title in each sentence. Circle the letters in the book titles that should be capitals.

**1.** I found a book with a long title. It's called <u>you can't take a balloon into the museum of fine arts</u>.

**2.** Another book is called <u>you can't take a balloon into the metropolitan museum</u>.

**3.** Read <u>discovering great artists</u> to learn how to draw like great artists.

**4.** My sister made a book. She called it <u>how to draw animals</u>.

**5.** I read a good book about a Chinese artist. It's called <u>the paper dragon</u>.

**6.** My brother should read the book called <u>how to draw batman</u>.

Choose a book title from the Word Bank to go with each sentence. Be sure to write the title correctly.

## Word Bank

| | |
|---|---|
| mole music | sing through the day |
| the cello of mr. o | meet the orchestra |
| fiddlin' sam | the farewell symphony |

**7.** A small animal changes the world with music in this book. **Mole Music**

**8.** If you like the cello, read this book. **The Cello of Mr. O**

**9.** To learn about instruments in an orchestra, read this book. **Meet the Orchestra**

**10.** If you feel like singing, this is the book for you. **Sing Through the Day**

**11.** This is the story of a boy who meets a special fiddler. **Fiddlin' Sam**

**12.** This book is about Joseph Haydn's last symphony. **The Farewell Symphony**

# Index of Skills

*a, an*, 51–52

abbreviations, 95–96

action verbs, 35–40, 59–66

adjectives, 41–44, 85–86
   *articles*, 51–52
   comparing with, 85–86

*and*, 45–46

articles, 51–52

*be*, forms of, 71–72

*but*, 45–46

capitalization
   initials and abbreviations, 95–96
   proper nouns, 29–30, 93–94
   sentences, 87–88, 99–100
   titles of books, 105–106
   titles of respect, 95

commands, 23–24

commas
   in a series, 101–102

common nouns, 27–28, 31–32

conjunctions, 45–46
   *coordinating*, 45–46

contractions, 97–98
   *it's*, 47–50
   *they're*, 53–56

end marks, 7, 19–26, 89–92, 99–100

exclamations, 23–26, 91–92, 99–100

fragments, 15–16

*I* or *me*, 83–84

irregular verbs, 59–66

*its* and *it's*, 47–50

naming yourself last, 83–84

nouns
   common, 27–28, 31–32
   proper, 29–32, 93–94
   singular and plural, 33–34

object pronouns, 79–80

*or*, 45–46

past tense verbs, 37–38, 73–76

plural nouns, 33–34

predicates
   complete, 9
   simple, 13–14

pronouns
   choosing the correct pronoun, 81–82
   *I, me*, 83–84
   naming yourself last, 83–84
   subjects and objects, 77–82

proper nouns, 29–32, 93–94

question marks, 19–22, 89–90, 99–100

quotation marks, 103–104

sentences
    capitalization, 87–88, 99–100
    commands and exclamations,
    23–26, 91–92, 99–100
    statements and questions,
    17–22, 89–90, 99–100
    subjects and predicates, 9–14
subject pronouns, 77–78, 81–82
subject-verb agreement, 67–70
subjects
    agreement with verbs, 67–70
    complete, 9–10
    simple, 11–12
*their, they're, there,* 53–58
titles
    of books, 105–106
    of respect, 95
verbs, 59–76
    action, 35–40, 59–66
    *be,* forms of, 71–72
    irregular, 59–66
    past tense, 37–38, 73–76
    present tense, 73–76

# Index of Topics
## Related to Content Areas

## Fine and Performing Arts

acting, 97–98

artists

Beatrix Potter, 94

Dr. Seuss, 95

Picasso, 93

books about Fine and Performing Arts, 105–106

dance

ballet, 103–104

music

instruments, 101–102

songs, 99–100

National Gallery of Art, 96

types of art

drawing, 87–88

painting, 89–90

sculpting, 91

statues, 92

## Language Arts

fables

"The Grasshopper and the Ant," 81–82

"The Hare and the Tortoise," 77–80, 86

"The Lion and the Mouse," 71–72, 85

fairy tales

"Cinderella," 73–76, 83, 85

"The Three Little Pigs," 67–68, 86

"The Ugly Duckling," 69–70

## Science/Animals

alligator, 27–28

antelope, 29–30

bear, polar, 39–40

crab, 45–46

dodo bird, 37–38

elephant, 55

giraffe, 55

grasshopper, 33–34

kangaroo, 61

koala, 61

lion, 55

newt, 41–42

owl, 35–36

puffer fish, 31–32

rabbit, 61

raccoon, 43–44

## Science/Geography

continents
>   Africa, 53, 55–56, 63
>   Antarctica, 49, 65–66
>   Asia, 53–54, 63
>   Australia, 61–62
>   Eurasia, 54
>   Europe, 54, 63–64
>   North America, 57–58
>   South America, 59–60

countries
>   Canada, 57
>   China, 53
>   Mexico, 57–58
>   Russia, 63–64
>   United States, 56, 63–64
>   Vatican City, 63
>   Venezuela, 60

lakes
>   Great Lakes, 58

lands
>   desert, 49
>   forest, 50
>   mountain, 47, 58, 60
>   plain, 47–49
>   rain forest, 50
>   tundra, 50
>   valley, 47–48

mountains, 47, 58
>   Andes, 60

oceans
>   Atlantic, 51, 58
>   Pacific, 51, 58

## Social Studies

Bethune, Mary McLeod, 13–14
Blackwell, Elizabeth, 9–10
Carver, George Washington, 7–8
Chavez, Cesar, 11–12
Jones, Frederick, 17–18
Jordan, Barbara, 19–20
Mott, Lucretia, 15–16
Muir, John, 21–22
Owens, Jesse, 25–26
Revere, Paul, 23–24